THE HEAVENLY VISION

Stephen Kaung

ISBN: 978-1-942521-39-6

Available from:

Christian Testimony Ministry
4424 Huguenot Road
Richmond, Virginia 23235

www.christiantestimonyministry.com

Printed in USA

CONTENTS

The first Northeast Christian Weekend Conference was held during October, 1988, at Long Beach Island, New Jersey. During this time, Stephen Kaung shared two messages on The Heavenly Vision. These spoken messages have been transcribed by permission into this book and edited only for clarity. Unless otherwise indicated, Scripture quotations are from the New Translation by J.N. Darby.

THE HEAVENLY VISION

Acts 26:19 Whereupon, king Agrippa, I was not disobedient to the heavenly vision.

Dear Heavenly Father, as we gather here together in the name of Thy beloved Son, our Lord Jesus Christ, we know that Thy presence is here with us. All we ask of Thee is Thou will put away any veil that may be upon our hearts that we may behold the glory of the Lord and be transformed from glory to glory according to His image as by the Lord, the Spirit. So Lord, we just ask Thee to grant us the Spirit of wisdom and revelation to the full knowledge of God. In the name of our Lord Jesus. Amen.

We do thank the Lord for giving us this time to be together. I feel that it is such a privilege for God's people to be together in the presence of our God and to encourage one another in the Lord because we are living in a very special time. I believe, brothers and sisters, we all have a sense in our spirit that the coming of the Lord is very imminent. He is nearer, probably, than what we think; even as the Scripture says, "He is at the doors." And because the coming of the Lord is so near, the morning is coming, but the night also comes. So in a sense, we are living at the darkest of the night before the day dawns, and it is very difficult during that hour for us to be kept watchful, alert, prepared, in tune with God and His purpose.

Before his martyrdom, the apostle Paul wrote to Timothy: "I have fought the good fight, I have finished the race, and I have kept the faith" (II Timothy 4:7). What a fight the apostle Paul had fought! He fought with the wild beasts in Ephesus. He fought against the unbelieving, idol- worshiping Gentiles. He fought against the unbelieving Jews. He fought against the Judaizers who tried to alter the truth of the gospel. He fought against the evil forces in the world. He fought against sin, flesh and the world. The apostle Paul fought with all that God had given to him. He received many wounds, but he fought on. He was a good warrior.

He really had run the race. On the road to Damascus, the Lord put him on that race. It was a marathon, an obstacle race, and yet the apostle Paul ran with patience, with endurance. In II Corinthians, chapters 6 and 11, you will find how he ran that race in many perils, often in prisons, in nakedness, in hunger, through honor and dishonor. He went through all those problems and difficulties with patience and endurance. He could declare towards the end that he had finished the race. Then, of course, we know how he kept the faith the faith that was once delivered to the saints. He had not given up any of the faith. The apostle Paul could declare towards the end of his life that he had fought the good fight, finished the race and kept the faith.

Brothers and sisters, do we have a less severe fight to fight? Do we have an easier race to run? Do we have less faith to keep? If we compare our days with the days of Paul, probably, we can say our days are even more difficult because we are approaching the end, and as the end is closing in, the days become more and more difficult. But then we need to ask ourselves: Have we fought the good fight? Have we finished the race? Have we kept the faith? Are we a good warrior for the Lord? Do we run with patience to the end? Have we compromised with the faith once delivered to the saints? So I think it is very urgent, very essential for us to consider together before the Lord how we can fight the good fight, finish the race, keep the faith in these last days. Is there any secret that enabled Paul to do so? And if there is such a secret, we would like to learn it.

If we want to use one sentence to sum up the life and ministry of the apostle Paul, I think it is that sentence that we read in the beginning: "King Agrippa, I was not disobedient to the heavenly vision." He could testify before King Agrippa that he was not disobedient to the heavenly vision. That explains him; that explains his life; that explains his ministry. It tells us the secret of how he was able to fight the good fight, finish the race and keep the faith.

WITHOUT VISION THE PEOPLE PERISH

Some of you brothers and sisters may be tired of hearing the word vision because we have talked about it

3

so many times. But you can call it whatever you want to. If you don't like the word vision, call it revelation. Or if you don't like the word revelation, call it purpose. If you don't like the word purpose, call it ambition. And if you don't like the word ambition, call it dream. You may call it whatever you want to, but you cannot escape it because this is a most fundamental, essential, vital, critical thing in our lives. Even in the natural world, no one can succeed without a vision, without a dream. If a person has no vision, no dream, no ambition, he is a drifter. He just drifts along with the current. He has no aim in his life and, because of this, no meaning to his life. A man without vision is a loser -he never succeeds; he is nobody, nothing, undistinguished, unknown. In whatever area in the world-whether it is political, economic, educational or even religious-if a person does not have a vision, a dream, he is a loser. Now if this is true in the natural world, how much more true it is in the spiritual world.

The wisest man in the world, Solomon, wrote in Proverbs 29:18 a verse that we are so familiar with: "Without vision, the people perish." Lance told us that the word perish in Hebrew simply means "to untie a knot" or "to unpin the hair and let the hair just fall down." In other words, without vision, people cast off restraint and become loose, with no discipline, no direction, no purpose; and because of this, they perish. This is very, very true.

4

PAUL'S VISION

In the spiritual world, it is essential that we have vision. Before the apostle Paul became Paul, he was Saul, and the man Saul was a man with vision. Even in the worldly sense, he was a man with dreams, with ambition. He wanted to be the Pharisee of the Pharisees, the Rabbi of the Rabbis; and because of this, he put himself into this task. Even though he was young, he was way ahead of his contemporaries, and he was on his way to becoming what he wanted to be: a man with ambition. But then, on the road to Damascus, he received the heavenly vision. A light shone upon him, and he fell to the ground. He heard a voice: "Saul, Saul, why do you persecute Me? It is hard for you to kick against the goads." And Saul said, "Lord, who are You?" The voice said, "I am Jesus of Nazareth whom you persecuted." Then Saul said, "Lord, what shall I do?" (see Acts 9).

Brothers and sisters, there on the road to Damascus, you find two visions in collision. Saul, the Pharisee, had a vision, an ambition, and he was on that course to fulfill it. But the heavens opened, the light came upon him, and a heavenly vision came to him in collision with his earthly vision. It finished Saul and created Paul.

When the heavenly vision comes, invariably, unavoidably, it finishes your earthly vision. If you say you have received the heavenly vision and yet you can continue on your course and do what you have planned to do, be what you want to be, then I have every reason to

5

doubt if you have received the heavenly vision because whenever the heavenly vision comes, it always destroys the earthly vision. You can never be the same, you can never do what you planned to do. It either changes your direction completely or it changes the very character of what you are involved with. It is so drastic, so revolutionary.

ONLY ONE VISION

What is a Christian? A Christian is a new creation. Old things have passed away; behold, all things have become new, and all things are of God. Regeneration, new birth is a great revolution. It revolutionizes your whole being. You cannot be what you were before because you are a new creation. Did such revolution come into your life when you believed in the Lord Jesus? How unfortunate it is that when we look back to the day we were saved, our direction may have shifted a little bit, but our course did not change. We have not been revolutionized as we should; we are not fully saved.

If you look into the Word of God, you find that people of faith are people with vision. Think of Noah. Noah received a revelation that the flood was coming, and God showed him the ark. Because of this revelation, the life of Noah was revolutionized. For 120 years, he became a shipbuilder. He was the first shipbuilder in the world because, before his time, there was no rain upon this earth. The vegetation was moistened by the moisture, the dew. Although there was no rain, yet you find Noah spent

120 years building that ark. He became the laughingstock of the world. People would come to him and say: "Noah, what are you doing? Why are you building that strange structure? Nobody has seen such a thing before." He would say to them that he was building an ark for the flood. "Now where is the rain?" They had never known what rain was. He became a preacher of righteousness. He preached, calling people to repent, to enter into the ark. He didn't succeed, and only his family was saved. But brothers and sisters, that made Noah what he was.

Think of Abraham. The Lord of glory appeared to him and, because of that, his whole life was changed. He could not stay in Ur of Chaldea, walking his familiar ground, being with his family; but he had to go out, not knowing where. But he knew God was calling him, and he lived the life of a pilgrim and stranger, living in tents.

Think of Moses. He saw the invisible One and that finished him up with the palace and all the riches in Egypt. He had to go with the Lord, bearing His reproach.

Think of the apostles in the early days. When the Lord called them, they left everything and followed the Lord. They saw the Lord, not just physically, because many people saw the Lord physically at that time. But John said: "We have contemplated His glory. We have seen His glory, even the glory of an only begotten with His Father" (see John 1:14). And when they saw the glory of the Lord in the Person of Jesus of Nazareth, they had to leave all and follow Him.

The same was true with the apostle Paul. The Lord met him and changed his course completely.

I remember when I was a high school student, thank God, many fellow students got saved. But I had a very close friend who was a classmate, and we tried to preach the gospel to him. He told us that if God would give him a vision like He had given to Paul, then he would believe. Unfortunately, so far as I can remember, that vision never came. He was killed in Hong Kong when the Japanese came. We may not be given exactly the same form, the same manner of that heavenly vision, and we should not expect that; but brothers and sisters, there is only one heavenly vision in the Scriptures. God has only one heavenly vision to give. It may come to people in different forms and different ways, according to their condition, but it is the same vision. The Scripture does not give us two visions or many visions. Now Paul does speak of visions and revelations in II Corinthians 12:1, but that is giving the details. So far as the supreme over-all vision from heaven is concerned, there is only one and one only.

Abel saw the better sacrifice. Noah saw the ark. Abraham saw the city with foundations. Moses saw the tabernacle. David saw the temple. Isaiah saw the Lord in the temple, high and lifted up. Daniel saw the coming King. Zechariah saw the golden lampstand with two olive trees standing by pouring gold into that lampstand. Peter saw a white sheet coming down from heaven, filled with beasts and creatures; and he heard a voice, "Kill and eat." Paul saw that heavenly Man, that universal Man -Christ,

8

the Head, in heaven, His body spread all over the world. John saw the seven lampstands with the Son of Man in the midst; and finally, he saw the New Jerusalem, the holy city descending from heaven. Are they different visions? You see a progression there. God revealed that vision to the world step by step, from the better sacrifice to the holy city, the new Jerusalem. You can see how it develops, how it grows.

Brothers and sisters, now we have the full vision revealed to us in the Word of God. Today, it is not a matter of how full that vision is; it is a matter of how much we see. The vision is there, but how much do we see of it? It is true, even in the life of the apostle Paul, that vision grew. On the road to Damascus, we may say he saw the framework, the outline of the heavenly vision. He saw Christ, the Head, with a body that covered not only Jerusalem and all the cities of Judea but even Samaria and Damascus. That was the beginning; and because he was faithful to what he saw, throughout his life that vision grew and developed. And this must be true with us today. We need, first of all, to see the outline of that heavenly vision. We need to have a vision of the framework of it, and then if we are faithful, the Lord will fill in all the details and make it full. This is essential.

CHRIST AND HIS CHURCH

What is that vision? If we want to put it in very plain words, that heavenly vision is none other but Christ and His church. No matter what kind of vision you see, what kind of ambition or dream you have, in essence, the heavenly vision is Christ and His church.

What is the earthly vision? In essence, the earthly vision is man and his own self. Think of Adam. He was ambitious; he wanted to be like God, and he could not wait. Because of this, he ate of the tree of knowledge of good and evil. He wanted to make himself God. Think of Nimrod. Probably, he was the first empire builder. He was the one who led that rebellion to build the tower of Babel that he might make a name for man, to exalt man. Think of Nebuchadnezzar. He built a huge, golden statue of man. He was that man. He was not satisfied with the revelation that God had given to him which was explained by Daniel that he was just a golden head. He wanted to be the whole man-ambitious. That is the earthly vision. No matter what your dream is, no matter what your ambition is, it comes down to one thing: you, self, man.

When you think of the heavenly vision, how different it is. That heavenly vision delivers us from the earth; it finishes man; it finishes you. It brings in Christ and the church. If you do not have that heavenly vision, you are still earth- bound, you are yet self-centered, you have not been uplifted out of this earth. But when the heavenly vision comes, it is so drastic it kills the natural man. That is the reason why many people have not received the heavenly vision or they have tried to escape the heavenly vision because it finishes their earthly vision. If you want to continue your own course, if you want to be what you planned to be, then avoid the heavenly vision.

I will mention our dear brother Watchman Nee. When he was a young man in school, he was very brilliant and he had lots of plans. He planned his future. He wanted to be something, somebody, to do something; and very likely, he would have succeeded. One day, he heard the gospel, and he knew it was true. He knew he was a sinner, and he knew that Christ was the Saviour, but he could not believe, he could not accept it because it cut across his ambition. He knew that if he should accept Jesus as his Saviour, he had to accept Jesus as his Lord. He had to give up himself, he had to give up his plans, he had to give up his earthly vision, his ambition, and capitulate it to Christ. He could not do that. He struggled with this matter for a few days, until one day, the love of Christ constrained him and he gave up himself. The Lord changed his course. Instead of being that which he wanted to be, he became a poor creature. Even his professor one day looked at him from top to bottom, shook his head and said: "What a pity. You could be somebody, but look at yourself now." Brothers and sisters, this is heavenly vision.

The whole Bible is just Christ and His church. Brother Nee told us, "If you see Christ and His church, the whole Bible is open to you." And how true it is. The Old Testament is types, shadows, representations; but where do you find the anti-types? Where is the substance? Where is the reality? When we read the Old Testament, if all we see are biographies of some great men and women, or the history of the children of Israel, or prophecies, or even the praises of the Psalms, then we have missed the point. We live in the shadow, not having the substance, and the shadow passes away. We live in the types and not in the reality.

Thank God, in the New Testament, the mystery of God is opened up and there you find, so plainly, Christ and His church. The gospels shows us Christ; Acts show us the history of the church, the story of Christ and His church; the epistles explain, teach, tell us what Christ is and what the church is; and the book of Revelation consummates in the New Jerusalem where Christ is all and in all. In the New Testament, it is so clear; but unfortunately, when people read the New Testament, all they see is just some more stories, some more histories, a religious organization called "Christianity" that seemed to be able to spread, some doctrines and teachings. Brothers and sisters, what a pity that we do not see Christ and His church in the Bible.

No wonder we cannot fight the good fight. As a matter of fact, if you do not have that heavenly vision, you have no fight to fight, you have no race to run, you have no faith to keep. That heavenly vision puts you in the fight. That is the reason why there are many Christians who do not know what spiritual warfare is. There is no warfare because there is no vision. They are no different from the world. They seek the things that the world is seeking. The world befriends them and they befriend the world. There is no fight. The enemy is not concerned about them. He can take his nap over them. There is no race to run because there is no direction. Vision gives us direction, gives us goals; and if you have no vision, there is no direction. You are like a child who is attracted by one thing at one time and the next minute he is attracted by another thing and off he goes. You will compromise with the faith to save your skin. It is only people with heavenly vision who are in the fight, who are in the race and who are in the faith. Vision gives us the strength to fight, the discipline to run, and the love to keep the faith. Brothers and sisters, I do not know how, I just look to the Lord that, by His Spirit, He would really impress upon your heart that without vision, you perish.

What is vision? You may say: "If I have no vision, then I am not saved. Surely I have seen Jesus as the Saviour." Thank God for that; you are saved. But that heavenly vision is more than just seeing the Lord Jesus as your Saviour. The heavenly vision is related to the eternal purpose of God. You may see Jesus as your Saviour, you may experience Him as your Comforter, or you may even know Him as your Supplier, but you are still lacking in the heavenly vision.

Let me illustrate. The children of Israel were slaves in Egypt; they were not allowed to live. But by the blood of the Paschal lamb, they were passed over, they did not die; and on the strength of the meat of the lamb, they started the heavenly pilgrimage. They crossed the Red Sea; they were baptized unto Moses; in the wilderness, God rained manna to feed them; and from the smitten rock, a river followed them through the wilderness to give them water. But they were a people who perished in the

13

wilderness not in Egypt, but in the wilderness. They failed to enter into the Promised Land. In other words, they did not arrive; they did not come into the purpose of God concerning them.

Brothers and sisters, this is the same with us today. Thank God, by the blood of the Lamb, our Lord Jesus, our sins are forgiven. Thank God that He has given us eternal life. Thank God, He has answered our prayers. Thank God, we were baptized unto Christ. Thank God, He supplies our every need; we know Him as our Supplier, our Comforter. But in spite of knowing all this, are we not still self-centered? Everything is Christ for me: He saved me; He supplies my needs. It is all me. It is not until you see the heavenly vision that you are delivered from me. You become Christ-centered. Therefore, the heavenly vision is not just any vision of Christ; it is the vision of Christ and His church in relation to the purpose of God. Unless we are united with God in Christ in His purpose, we remain babes in Christ.

CHRIST AS HEAD

That heavenly vision is what Christ tells us He is. What does He tell us about Himself? Of course, we can only try to sum up; otherwise, we will have to start eternity from now. There is one passage in the Scripture that I feel, in a sense, will sum up what Christ is in the eternal purpose of God.

14

Fear not; I am the first and the last, and the living one: and I became dead, and behold, I am living to the ages of ages, and have the keys of death and of hades. (Revelation 1:17-18)

Here, our Lord Jesus declared Himself to His beloved disciple, the apostle John. John had known the Lord so intimately when He was on earth; yet when he saw the Lord in glory, he fell as one dead. And then the Lord said: "Fear not; I will tell you who I am. I will tell you what I am in the eternal purpose of God." Of course, John knew the Lord Jesus as the Saviour, His Master, no doubt about that. But here the Lord Jesus said, "I am the first." What does that mean?

You remember in Colossians 1, it says that it is God's will that Christ shall have the pre-eminence in all things. The will of God is that Christ should have the first place in all things. He shall have the priority. He is the beginning. He must be first in all things. In all things in your life-whether it is in your personal life, your family life, your church life or your social life-Christ has to be first. It is easy to say, "Lord, You are the first"; but it is very difficult when it comes down to daily life. Is Christ really the first in your affection? the first in your thought? the first in all things that you do? Do you have your plan and then ask Him to put His stamp on it? Or do you allow Him to show you His plan for you? Brothers and sisters, this is the heavenly vision. A person who has seen the heavenly vision has to let Christ be the first.

In the gospels, the Lord challenged the disciples again and again: "Unless you deny yourself, take up your cross and follow Me, you cannot be My disciple. If you love your father and mother, brother and sister, wife and children, and even your own life more than Me, you cannot be My disciple." This is not related to initial salvation; this is related to the heavenly vision. Christ has to be first. This is God's will.

He also has to be the last because all the purpose of God is summed up in Him, all the fulfillment of God's plan is in Him. He must be the last. In other words, does He have the last word in your life? The last word in the church? In the early days, when the church in Jerusalem had a problem with Antioch, they came together and discussed it. You can discuss, but who has the last word? The Holy Spirit-He is the last. It means that all glory goes back to Him; all things are from Him, through Him and unto Him; to Him be glory forever. Amen. Is that true? He is the first and the last and all in between. That is what the Scripture says: "He is all and in all." Brothers and sisters, that is the heavenly vision.

He said, "I am the living one." He is life, the originator of life, the life-giving Spirit. If you have anything to do with Christ, it has to be life. It is not just teaching or doctrine, how-ever accurate it may be. It is not just form, however orthodox it may be. It is life.

Is your relationship with Christ a life relationship? Is the church relationship with Christ a life relationship? He

16

says, "I am the living one; and that is what I am giving-life." In Him was life and the life was the light of man. Anything that is not life is not of God; it is not of Christ; it is tradition.

"Behold, I became dead." That is the work of Christ. He came into this world to die. He does not need to die, nor can He die as God. But He came as a Man to die in order to save us mortals and destroy death. He entered into death; He swallowed up death with His life and He came out in resurrection. Anything that has to do with Christ in that eternal purpose of God has to be on the ground of resurrection. Whatever is not on resurrection ground is not of God, is not in the purpose of God. It has to be on resurrection ground.

"I hold the keys of death and of hades." His victory is so complete that now He holds the keys of death and of hades. This is the eternal purpose of God concerning Christ. This is what Christ is to us. Do we know Him as such? Do we catch a glimpse of what Christ is? He is much greater than we think. Brother Sparks used to say, "You make Christ small." And how true it is; we do. May the Lord enlarge our vision.

CHRIST AS THE BODY

What is the church in the eternal purpose of God? It is not just a gathering of the saints, that is to say, not a religious gathering of the world. It is more than that. And I think another two verses probably can sum it up.

And has put all things under his feet, [that is, under the feet of Christ] and gave him to be head over all things to the church, which is his body, the fulness of him who fills all in all. (Ephesians 1:22-23)

Brothers and sisters, the church is so much bigger than what people think today. It says here that Christ is Head over all things to the church, which is His body, the fulness of Him who fills all in all. First of all, the church is the body of Christ. Christ is the Head, the church is His body. All the intelligence, all the control, all the wisdom, all the riches, all the directions are in the Head; and that Head is joined with a body. In other words, the body is to inherit, to contain all that the Head is and to manifest the Head. That is the church. The Head and the body are one; and that is the reason why the risen Head said, "Saul, why do you touch Me?" It was because he touched members of His body. There is a unity, a oneness between the Head and the body. The body contains all the riches of the Head and is under the headship of Christ. The body is to manifest all the glory of the Head. Today, the world does not see the Head but they do see the body, and through the body, they see the Head. That is what the church is.

What is the church? It says that God has made Christ Head over all things to the church. Christ is not only the Head of the church, He is Head over all things to the church. I think this means at least two things. One thing is that Christ is the Head over all things. The other is that He has controlled and overcome all things, and He has given that victory to the church that the church may be above

18

all things, that the church may find all things working together for good, that the church may subdue all things to Christ. The church is to enjoy all that Christ is as Head over all things. That is the reason, in Romans, chapter 8, Paul gives a song of victory, a triumphant song: "Who can separate us from the love of God which is in Christ Jesus? If God is for us, who can be against us?" Is there anything in earth, under the earth, now or in the future, anything that can separate us from God? No, because Christ is Head over all things to the church. And not only that, but we become the instrument in God's hands to bring all things back to Christ because it is the will of God to sum up all things in Christ. That is the purpose of God.

Brothers and sisters, this is the heavenly vision, and it ought to destroy any earthly ambition in us; it ought to finish us, as it were. That heavenly vision ought to uplift us to heaven, enlarge our capacity and humble us, seeing how little we know of that heavenly vision. But we need that framework, that outline; and if we have received that outline, if we are faithful, God will fill it into fulness until we find, truly, the church is the body of Christ, the fulness of Him who fills all and in all. So may the Lord have mercy upon us.

Dear Heavenly Father, we do feel ourselves as little children playing with pebbles by the seashore. We do not know how vast, how deep is the ocean. Oh, how we praise and thank Thee because Thou are great, and the heavenly vision that Thou has so graciously given to Thy church through the centuries is beyond our comprehension; but we do praise and thank Thee, it is not beyond our reach. Thou has given it to Thy church and, Lord, we want to see it, we want to be involved in it, we want to be part of it. So Lord, we just humble ourselves before Thee and say: Give us vision that we may see Christ and the church, that we may be delivered from ourselves, that we may be delivered from individualism, that we may be delivered into Christ and into the church. And to Thee be the glory. We ask in the name of our Lord Jesus. Amen.

NOT DISOBEDIENT TO THE HEAVENLY VISION

Acts 26:13-23 - At mid-day, on the way, I saw, O king, a light above the brightness of the sun, shining from heaven round about me and those who were journeying with me. And, when we were all fallen to the ground, I heard a voice saying to me in the Hebrew tongue, Saul, Saul, why persecutest thou me? it is hard for thee to kick against goads. And I said, Who art thou, Lord? And the Lord said, I am Jesus whom thou persecutest: but rise up and stand on thy feet; for, for this purpose have I appeared to thee, to appoint thee to be a servant and a witness both of what thou hast seen, and of what I shall appear to thee in, taking thee out from among the people, and the nations, to whom I send thee, to open their eyes, that they may turn from darkness to light, and from the power of Satan to God, that they may receive remission of sins and inheritance among them that are sanctified by faith in me. Whereupon, king Agrippa, I was not disobedient to the heavenly vision; but have, first to those both in Damascus and Jerusalem, and to all the region of Judea, and to the nations, announced that they should repent and turn to God, doing works worthy of repentance. On account of these things the Jews, having seized me in the temple, at-tempted to lay hands on and destroy me. Having therefore met with the help which is from God, I have stood firm unto this day, witnessing both to small and great, saying nothing else than those things which both the prophets and Moses have said should happen, namely, whether Christ should suffer; whether he first, through resurrection of the dead, should announce light both to the people and to the nations.

Dear Heavenly Father, we offer the word that Thou has given to us back to Thee and ask that Thou will bless Thy word, break it and distribute it to us that we may be filled, that Thou may be glorified and Thy will be done among us upon earth as it is in heaven. We ask in Thy precious name. Amen.

We have been sharing together on this matter of the heavenly vision. The heavenly vision is not optional; it is mandatory. In other words, as God's people, we must have this heavenly vision because, without it, we perish; we cast off all restraint, we become a people without discipline. Without this vision, we will be divided and scattered. There will be no unity, no cohesion among God's people. It is this heavenly vision that gives us purpose and meaning. It is this heavenly vision that satisfies God's own heart; and only that vision can satisfy our longing hearts. So it is essential that we, as the redeemed of the Lord, have this vision.

It is the vision that is related to the eternal purpose of God, and it is not a small thing. It is a vision of Christ as all and in all. It is a vision of the church as the body of Christ, the fulness of Him who fills all and in all. But God does not give such vision just for us to contemplate, to meditate and to think about. Our God is very practical. The reason why He gives such vision to His people is because He wants to work out something for His glory.

We have to see that this heavenly vision is not just some-thing objective, although there is the objective aspect of it that God has given to us in Christ Jesus through the Holy Spirit. It is something that we need to see with our inner eyes. But this vision is more than just something objective for us to view from afar. It is a vision that is also very subjective. When it is given, it draws us in and makes us part of the vision, and we cannot help but be involved fully and completely in it.

VOCATION

Vision is given for vocation; and if it is not for vocation, then there is no meaning to that vision. We remember the case with the apostle Paul. When he was on the road to Damascus, he was given the heavenly vision. It had to be accepted by faith, and it resulted in a commitment and ended up with a com-mission. It is not something vague nor is it something abstract; it is something most practical and it touches our very life upon this earth. It revolutionizes our life and it revolutionizes our ministry. It is for a vocation.

Probably, we have the thought of how glorious it would be if we were given such a vision. And it is true, because this heavenly vision is the most glorious thing in the universe. There is nothing more glorious than seeing the purpose of God concerning Christ and His church because it lifts us up out of ourselves, out of this world, delivers us from this earth and makes us heaven-bound. It really gets us into His glory. That vision is most glorious.

UNFIT FOR THE VISION

At the same time, this heavenly vision is most terrible. You remember the story of Jacob. He did have a spiritual desire. He did desire spiritual things, even though he was a carnal man. He tried to attain spiritual reality through carnal means; and of course, we know he could not. Because of this, he was so disciplined that he had to leave home. He wandered in the wilderness and at night he laid his head upon a stone as his pillow. I think you can hardly describe a more pitiful, tragic scene than this young man, worn out, with his head on the stone, asleep. At that time, God revealed Himself to him. He saw a ladder that connected the earth and heaven. God was on the top of that ladder, and Jacob was lying at the bottom of that ladder with angels ascending and descending on it. God said to him: "I am the God of your father; I am with you. I will perform all that I have promised to your father, Abraham, and to Isaac." Jacob woke up, and do you know what he said? "Oh, this is wonderful, this is marvelous!" No; his reaction was, "This is terrible. This is a terrible place because this is the house of God, the gate of heaven." Why was it so terrible? It was terrible because he found himself so unfit, so unworthy. He found himself so far from what the vision was, and he knew it was a terrible thing. If this is true, how much must be done in his life! It was terrible!

Nevertheless, as terrible as it was to him, he accepted it, even though he did not understand fully. We know that even after that vision, he still bargained with God. God said, "I am with You"; and he said, "If You are with me." God said, "I will bless you with all the blessings of Abraham"; and he said, "If You will give me clothes to wear and food to eat and keep me safe, then I will make You my God." He still bargained with God; he did not understand fully what that vision was. Yet on the other hand, he did accept it because he put up that stone to be a pillow, he poured oil on it and he said, "If God will fulfill all this, I will make this the house of God."

Dear brothers and sisters, on the one hand, he saw it was a terrible thing because he found himself so far away from that vision, and he knew to be made fit for that vision would take a long road. Yet he did commit himself to God and allow God to work it out in his life, to make him the house of God. He poured oil on the stone. Symbolically, it means by the power of the Holy Spirit, it shall be done. And because he accepted that vision with faith-however imperfect that faith might have been -because he did commit himself to God's hand, from that day onward, the hand of God was upon that man. For twenty years, God worked in his life, trying to break him down, trying to remake him; but he was such a strong person. It took God twenty years (and through a man with a similar nature) to deal with this man Jacob until, finally, God broke him and trans-formed him from Jacob to Israel, a prince with God.

Whenever the heavenly vision comes upon a person, the first reaction is how unfit, unworthy he is. You remember the prophet Isaiah. If you read the first few chapters of Isaiah, you find what a strong prophet he was. He denounced; he announced judgment to God's people as if he was above the people. Yet in the sixth chapter, when his close friend king Uzziah died, he went into the temple; and in a vision, he saw the Lord upon the throne, highly lifted up, His train filling the temple. Seraphim were crying out, "Holy, holy, holy, Lord God Almighty; the whole earth is full of His glory." And the house was filled with smoke and there was shaking. This strong prophet cried out, "Woe unto me! for I am undone; for I am a man of unclean lips, and I dwell in the midst of a people of unclean lips" (Isaiah 6:5). There is no member of the body of a prophet stronger than the lips because he is a spokesman of God. He uses his mouth, his lips; that is his strength. Yet when he saw the Lord on the throne, his strength turned into weakness. He discovered how unclean his lips were. He was not fit to speak for God. It is only people who have no vision who feel they are fit to speak for God. If you see God, you dare not speak; you know how unclean your lips are. But thank God, he was cleansed by the fire from the altar; and from that day onward, he became the spokesman of God to His people.

The same thing happened to the prophet Ezekiel. In Ezekiel, chapter 1, when the glory of the Lord appeared to him, he fell down. He could not stand any more. It also happened to Daniel, the beloved of God. In Daniel, chapter 10, when the Lord appeared to him in glory, he fell down as one dead and said, "My glory, my beauty has turned into corruption." We know that Daniel was the beloved of God. He was such a perfect man. In the Bible, a few people are mentioned without any fault. It is not that they had no fault, but it is not mentioned; and Daniel is one of them. Yet when he saw the Lord, his beauty turned into corruption.

Dear brothers and sisters, if we say we have seen the heavenly vision and it only makes us think we are worthy, we are fit instead of making us see our unworthiness, our total unfitness, I wonder whether we have seen the heavenly vision. The first reaction that comes to a person who has seen the Lord is to find himself so unworthy, so unfit, he has to fall down as dead; and he has to rely upon the Lord to raise him up from the dead.

OBEDIENCE TO THE VISION

Whenever a vision comes, it demands obedience. Do not think a vision is given just to make you feel good or just to make you think that you are more spiritual than other people. The apostle Paul could testify, "I was not disobedient to the heavenly vision."

I wonder why he used double negatives. Why did he not say, "King Agrippa, I was obedient to the heavenly vision?" It would have been much simpler to say that and more positive. But he said, "I was not disobedient to the heavenly vision." Now I know in the Hebrew language, sometimes you use double negatives to make it more emphatic; but personally, I believe there must be something more. Is it not that Paul sensed, very deeply, out of his experience through many years, that obedience was simply something not in him? On the contrary, he found that disobedience was in him. In other words, the very nature of the old man is disobedience.

When the first man Adam disobeyed God, it seems that in the very blood of Adam there was disobedience; and we who are the descendants, the seeds of Adam, discover that within us there is that seed of disobedience. Disobedience is not just an act occasionally. We discover that disobedience is deeply implanted in our very natural life. It is easy for us to disobey; it is very difficult for us to obey. Even in this world, you will discover that when a child begins to talk, the first thing he says is no. It is very difficult for a child to say yes because the very spirit of disobedience is in that natural life. Unless we see this, we are not delivered. We have to acknowledge that, in our spirit, that is in the fallen man, there is the very spirit of rebellion, of disobedience, especially when you come to the things of God. Some people may be quite obedient outwardly, but it may not be true inwardly. And if you find it is hard to obey in the natural sense, how much more difficult it is to obey God, to obey that heavenly vision. It is not there.

Do not think it was easy for Paul to obey after seeing such a glorious vision or obedience became something natural to him; it was not so. If you read Paul's writings, you will find again and again where he said the mind of the flesh does not understand the things of God. He said the carnal mind cannot accept God's will because it is folly to him; the man of the flesh cannot please God. Brothers and sisters, these are not just words; these are experiences. Out of his own experience, he discovered that, in him, that is in the flesh, there is no obedience. And I think that is the reason why he said, "I was not disobedient." Naturally, he would be disobedient to the heavenly vision; but supernaturally, he was not disobedient.

The heavenly vision demands obedience; but remember, in you there is no such thing as obedience, especially when you come to the heavenly vision because with the heavenly vision comes the cross. It is the cross that converts that vision into vocation. If the vision is given and there is no cross, you become a visionary. But God does not give a vision to make you a visionary; God gives vision that it may be a vocation to you. And in order that it be a vocation, with the vision comes the cross. Therefore, it is terrible.

Think of our Lord Jesus. He is the heavenly vision; but for Him to be that heavenly vision, even before the foundation of the world, He was the Lamb slain. When He came into this world, it was not easy as it was when we came, because He had to empty Himself. He was God; He was equal with God. He received all the worship, the adoration, the praises, the service of the angelic hosts. That was His right. In order to complete that vision, He had to empty Himself. It is true, He could never empty Himself of His deity because even though He became man, He was still God. But He emptied Himself of all that surrounded His deity-His honor, His glory, His rights, His authority. He laid down everything. He emptied Himself in order to become a Man. That is the cross.

As a Man, how He denied Himself! If there is any man that does not need to deny Himself, it was our Lord Jesus because even His human self was pure, sinless, perfect. And yet He denied Himself to the point that He said: "I cannot do anything by Myself. I cannot say anything by Myself. I cannot. Your time is always easy, but My time is not yet come." His whole life was a life of the cross. He denied Himself to the point that He entered into death, and even the death of the cross. We can never understand fully what He suffered nor how much He suffered throughout His life. We can never fully understand how much suffering He suffered on Calvary's cross. He not only suffered physically, He suffered mentally, He suffered spiritually. He had to give up everything. He had to lay down His life. He had to cry out, "My God, My God, why hast Thou forsaken Me?"

Yet it was through the things which He suffered that He learned obedience. Our Lord Jesus learned obedience while He was on earth. As God, obedience was not in His vocabulary. God never needs to obey. God commands. So our Lord Jesus as Man, as God-Man, had to learn a new lesson; He had to learn obedience, and it was through the things which He suffered. How much He suffered! How much He had to deny His holy self! How much He had to lay down His holy life! But from the things which He suffered, He learned obedience and He became the author of our eternal salvation. One translation says (and it is more accurate): "He became the cause of our eternal salvation" (Hebrews 5:9). In other words, He learned obedience not for Himself; He learned obedience in His life for us because He is going to give His own life to us, and in that life there is the spirit of obedience.

We can never obey God; we can never obey the heavenly vision by ourselves. But thank God, today there is the possibility, there is the potential, because in the very life that we receive from our Lord Jesus when we believe in Him, there is obedience. It is only by that life that Paul said, "I was not disobedient to the heavenly vision." Do not think that you can obey the heavenly vision. If anybody should think that he or she can obey the heavenly vision or he or she can even make it work, they deceive themselves. They have not seen the vision; or they have turned away from the vision and they are building something else. If God, by His mercy, should give us that heavenly vision, we have to humbly acknowledge

31

it is totally out of us, beyond us; it is something we cannot fulfill. But thank God, by that life, it can be done.

That heavenly vision either makes us or breaks us. When that heavenly vision comes to us, we find it demands obedience. Yet within us, in our flesh, we find there is rebellion; we just cannot obey. We find that it demands too much because it demands our very life; it demands all. And we know that it means that we have to deny ourselves, take up the cross and follow the Lord; but we find that we cannot do it. If we try to struggle to do it on our own, it breaks us. But if, by the mercy of God, we realize that we cannot make it but He can, then He will make us.

CAPTURED BY THE VISION

The heavenly vision is such a strange thing. On the one hand, it repels us, and on the other hand, it attracts us. Let me illustrate it. You remember the story of Peter. When he was brought to the Lord by his brother Andrew, the Lord looked at him (see John 1:42). In the original, it means the Lord looked him over, up and down; and evidently, the look of the Lord just penetrated into the very heart of Peter. Peter was a very talkative person. He always spoke first; yet when he was brought to the Lord and the Lord looked him over, he was speechless. He never uttered a word; and the Lord said, "You are Simon weak as water but you shall be Peter, firm as a stone." Peter followed the Lord.

The Lord called Peter when he was fishing: "Come and follow Me, and I will make you a fisher of men." Peter left his boat, left his net and followed the Lord. And you remember in the very early days Peter began to travel with the Lord and spend time with Him. But one day, when our Lord Jesus went to Capernaum, Peter's home town, you find Peter went fishing (see Luke 5). Now why did he go fishing? He had left his boat and fish net to follow the Lord, and now he went back to fishing. But God did not allow him to catch a single fish. Suppose he had succeeded?

In the morning, the Lord borrowed his boat to preach and He said: "If that is what you want to do, I am borrowing your boat and I will pay you the price. Go out, put down the net; you will catch fish to pay for your boat if that is the way you want to deal with Me." The net was full of fishes. What was the reaction of Peter? Peter fell down before the Lord and said: "Depart from me, I am a sinful man. I am not worthy." Peter thought he could make it. He was attracted by the Lord and he followed the Lord, but after spending time with the Lord, he discovered that he was an unfit; he could not make it. So he felt it was better to slip out early, and that is why he went fishing. But the Lord revealed to Peter His glory as the Creator. He had command over the whole universe; and when Peter saw the glory of the Lord in that net full of fishes, his reaction was: "Depart from me, I am a sinful man."

Do you think you are fit for the Lord? Do you think you are fit for the heavenly vision? You are not fit. You will cry out within you, "Depart from me, Lord, I am a sinful man." It repels you. The heavenly vision repels you, and yet on the other hand, it draws you. Even though Peter said, "Depart from me," in his heart he was crying out, "Lord, if you are merciful to me, don't let me go."

In John, chapter 6, what a difference we see. After the Lord had fed five thousand with five fishes and two loaves, the people wanted to make the Lord King. He retreated to the other side of the lake and the people followed Him. The Lord said: "Seek not the things that perish but the things that are eternal. I am the bread of life." And when our Lord said these things, His disciples said, "It is a hard saying"; and many departed from Him. The twelve disciples were there and the Lord turned to them and said: "Do you want to go? If you do, you may." And Peter said: "Where can we go? To whom shall we go? We are finished. You have the Word of life; You are the holy One of God. We are stuck with You." That is the heavenly vision. If you see the heavenly vision, you have now-here else to go. Many times I have tried to go away, but there was nowhere to go. Dear brothers and sisters, if you still have an alternative, you have not seen the vision. People who have seen the vision are finished with everything. We are stuck with Christ forever. There is no other place to go, no other one to go to; He has captured us. We are caught forever.

COMPROMISING THE VISION

When this heavenly vision comes to us, there is the temptation. On the one hand, we want to obey; but on the other hand, we find it is hard to obey. During that time, there is a great temptation to compromise that vision. It was so even with the father of faith, Abraham. When the Lord of glory appeared to him, the call came: "Depart from your homeland, from your kindred, from your father's house and go to the place of My choice." Abraham obeyed, but he compromised. In Genesis 11, you find that it was not Abraham who went out, it was his father Terah who brought Abraham out with his wife and with his nephew Lot. In other words, when God appeared to Abraham, he desired to obey, but he compromised. He let his father take the initiative and he brought out Lot, too. They came to the land of Haran in the middle of Ur and the Promised Land, and there he stopped; he compromised. And when a vision is com-promised, God becomes silent. During those days in Haran, God never appeared to Abraham again.

Brothers and sisters, is this your story? Once upon a time, God did appear to you. Your eyes were opened and you saw Christ. He deserves the first place. You saw the church as the fulness of Christ and you were attracted by it. But then you considered your way and you compromised. The result was you fell into darkness. It was only by the mercy of God that the way was opened for Abraham. It was very tragic; God took away Terah. But then God appeared to him again and said the very same thing. There was no new vision, no addition; it was the same old vision because he had not obeyed. He had compromised.

Oh brothers and sisters, what a temptation it is to compromise God's vision. And when God's vision is compromised, gradually, it becomes dimmer and dimmer and dimmer until it becomes something of the past. You may be able to look back and say, "Five years ago, God appeared to me;" but you live in the past; you are not in the present nor in the future.

OBEDIENCE OR SACRIFICE

In I Samuel 15:22, God spoke through Samuel to Saul: "Obedience is better than sacrifice." There is another temptation. When the heavenly vision comes to us, our response is to substitute sacrifice for obedience. We are very clever. We do not want to obey because we know we will have to allow the cross to work in our lives. We want to keep our integrity. Therefore, we offer sacrifice to God: "I will do this for You, I will do that for You. I will offer sacrifice to You."

Let me use an illustration, again, of our brother Watchman Nee. He grew up with the Chang family; and from his youth, he fell in love with one of Chang's girls, Charity. They had a mutual agreement, an understanding that they would become one; and then brother Nee got saved. After he got saved, of course, he was very concerned about Charity; so he tried to talk to her about the Lord and lead her to Christ. If he should succeed, then the earthly vision and the heavenly vision would go in the same way; but God did not honor that. You know what brother Nee did? He bargained with God. He said: "Lord, if You let me have her, I am willing to go anywhere You want me to go. I will serve You." But our God does not seek a bargain. Finally, our brother yielded; he changed his clothes, put on an old gown, made some paste and went out to the streets and put up scriptural posters. That was his declaration; he was dead to the world. The Scripture that spoke to him was: "Whom have I in the heavens? and there is none upon earth I desire beside thee" (Psalm 73:25). He could say, "I have no one in heaven but Thee, Lord", but he could not say before that he did not desire anybody else on earth except the Lord. But from that day onward, he was able to follow the vision that God had given to him. After many years of separation, God, in His sovereignty, saved Charity and finally they became husband and wife.

However, what I want to emphasize is that, oftentimes, when the heavenly vision comes to us, we try to substitute obedience with sacrifice. Do you think God wants your sacrifice? Do you think God really wants your service? Do you think your sacrifice can satisfy His heart if He does not have you? if He does not have your obedience? No; obedience is better than sacrifice. Often, when a person sees a vision, instead of being open to God in the attitude of obedience and letting God work out that vision in his life and through his life, he hurries off and tries to work it out. When you do that, you create a monster. What God wants in us is obedience, not sacrifice.

The heavenly vision is very sensitive. It can easily be clouded, it can easily be lost, it can easily be distracted into something else. We find many of God's people have had a vision in the beginning, but they are being distracted into something else.

THE WHEEL

I would like to use an example-a wheel. A wheel is a tremendous invention; and in the Bible, you find the wheel is also very important, especially in Ezekiel, where you find the wheel within the wheel. The heavenly vision is like a wheel, which speaks of motion, the movement of God, moving towards a goal. The center of this wheel-the axle-is Christ, and the rim is the church. Then all the other things-whether they are truth or experiences-all these things that you find in the Bible are the spokes. They all center upon Christ and reach out to the church. Or to put it another way, everything you find in the Scripture, everything you find in life, every truth, every experience are all spokes. They have to come out from Christ, the center, and they reach to the church as the rim. That is the way the wheel moves. So everything is related to Christ and comes out to the church.

Our problem is that instead of seeing the heavenly vision as a wheel, we lose our vision of the center or we lose the vision of the rim and all we see is a spoke here and a spoke there. Now these spokes represent truth, not false doctrines. These spokes represent spiritual experience, not just something mystical. But whenever a truth is seen out of the context of Christ and the church, it becomes a thing by itself. It becomes a substitute of the heavenly vision. And many people, today, are being occupied with some of these spokes.

All of these spokes are off balance. You have to balance these spokes with Christ on one end and the church on the other end. When a truth or experience is out of the context of Christ and the church, it is either too short or too long; the wheel will either break or you will just jerk around; and that is what is happening today. Dear brothers and sisters, we need to center on Christ and we need to have the church as the boundary. Then you will find the church as the body of Christ, the fulness of Him who fills all and in all.

Dear Heavenly Father, will You please, in Your mercy, reveal that heavenly vision to Thy redeemed people? Will you please, by Thy grace, make us faithful that we, with our brother Paul, may declare we are not disobedient to the heavenly vision? Will You please bring that vision to us and bring us into that vision? Will You please glorify Thyself and Thy beloved Son? Lord, we offer ourselves to Thee. We are at Thy disposal. Do whatever Thou does seem fit with us. We acknowledge that we are totally unfit but, Lord, Thou are able to make us fit to that vision; and for this we are grateful. We ask in the name of our Lord Jesus. Amen.

www.ingramcontent.com/pod-product-compliance
Lightning Source LLC
Chambersburg PA
CBHW060631030426
42337CB00018B/3310